"Bring The Classics To Life"

SEA WOLF

LEVEL 3

Series Designer
Philip J. Solimene

Editor
Laura Machynski

EDCON
Long Island, New York

Story Adaptor
Carolyn Gloeckner

Author
Jack London

Historical Background

In days of old, the hunting of seals was common practice. The seals were hunted for their skins (soft, silky fur), which made excellent coats, and provided a good source of income when traded at markets.

The meat of the seal, though not tasty, was, nevertheless, considered a good food source, and seal blubber (fat) was used for cooking, or was burned to provide light and heat.

Seals were hunted for hundreds of years. When their numbers had been severely reduced to the point of becoming extinct, many nations, including the United States, signed treaties to limit the hunting of this animal.

Seals are still hunted today, but thanks to conservation measures, their population has risen to about 1.3 million, most of which originate on the Probilof Islands (about 300 miles off the southwestern coast of Alaska), under the watchful eye of the U.S. Fish and Wildlife Service.

Copyright © 1994
A/V Concepts Corp.
Long Island, New York

Printed in U.S.A.
ISBN 1-55576-180-1

CONTENTS

Words Used 4, 5

WORDS USED

Story 61	Story 62	Story 63	Story 64	Story 65
KEY WORDS				
deck	cabin	expect	drank	bunk
faint	course	fellow	knife	ocean
fog	force	lie	repeat	search
journey	learn	neither	sharp	shape
passenger	lesson	pot	strike	slept
rescue	sailor	reply	wouldn't	you've
NECESSARY WORDS				
captain	died	galley	job	beat
life preserver	dry	scold	pour	murderer
pilot-house	gentleman	spill	shake	oilskins
ship	hatch	staterooms	swabs	worthless
	seal	tea	whiskey	

WORDS USED

Story 66	Story 67	Story 68	Story 69	Story 70

KEY WORDS

Story 66	Story 67	Story 68	Story 69	Story 70
coffee	breeze	certainly	island	kiss
curl	sank	gentle	prepare	leak
sail	steer	happiness	raise	match
slide	trap	joy	saving	needle
spray	weather	respect	tire	softly
tumble	welcome	wrote	wore	somebody

NECESSARY WORDS

Story 66	Story 67	Story 68	Story 69	Story 70
hated	hundred	argue	bail	body
jib	mend	earn	cove	chest
masts	raged	fade	gun	handcuff
rigging		meal	load	hut
		newspaper	sick	
			trust	

Out of the Fog

PREPARATION

Key Words

deck	(dek)	the floor of a boat *We walked across the <u>deck</u> together.*
faint	(fānt)	not loud; soft *The bird made a <u>faint</u> sound as it landed on the roof.*
fog	(fog)	a cloud near the ground *They could not see the flag because of the <u>fog</u>.*
journey	(jėr´ nē)	a trip from one place to another *The people went on a long <u>journey</u> to a new land.*
passenger	(pas´ en jėr)	someone who is riding on a boat, plane, train, car, or bus *Mark was the only <u>passenger</u> on the bus.*
rescue	(res´ kü)	to save, take or move away from danger *When Lee's boat turned over, his friends came to <u>rescue</u> him.*

Out of the Fog

Necessary Words

captain   (kap´ tən)   a person who runs a ship
The <u>captain</u> told his men what to do.

life preserver (līf´ pri zėrv´ ər)   a jacket or vest worn to keep people from drowning
You must wear a <u>life</u> <u>preserver</u> in the water if you can't swim well.

pilot-house   (pī´lət hous´)   a place high up on the deck of a ship where the captain can look out
The captain watched the stormy sea from the <u>pilot-house</u>.

ship   (ship)   a large boat
The <u>ship</u> sailed across the sea.

People

Humphrey van Weyden   is a man taking a trip on a boat.

Things

Martinez   is the name of a ship in this story.

Out of the Fog

It was not a good day for a sea journey.

Preview: 1. Read the name of the story.
2. Look at the picture.
3. Read the sentence under the picture.
4. Read the first two paragraphs of the story.
5. Then answer the following question.

You learned from your preview that Humphrey van Weyden
___a. was on his way to work.
___b. was on his way home.
___c. did not like the sea.
___d. did not like the fog.

Turn to the Comprehension Check on page 10 for the right answer.

Now read the story.

Read to find out what happens to Humphrey at sea.

Out of the Fog

Humphrey van Weyden was going home. He was a passenger on a ship, the *Martinez*.

Fog had rolled in, so it was not a good day for a sea journey. Humphrey stood on the deck and looked at the fog. He could not see the sky or the sea. Everything, everywhere, was gray.

Another passenger walked out onto the deck and stopped to talk to Humphrey.

He said, "There's danger out there. There are too many ships about. We can't see them and they can't see us. Listen — do you hear them?"

Humphrey listened. He could hear bells that sounded faint and far away. Others sounded close. There were whistles, too. Some were loud, some soft. Behind him, he could hear the *Martinez's* whistle blowing loudly.

"Those bells and whistles are telling us where other ships are," said the man.

One far-off whistle became louder. The *Martinez* slowed. A few minutes passed. The whistle became still louder. The men could hear the other ship pass to one side. The whistle grew faint again. At last, they heard it no more.

"Hello! I hear a ship coming up fast!" the other passenger said. He looked up at the pilot-house, where the captain stood. Humphrey turned around, too. The captain was white-faced. He looked frightened. He looked as if he were trying to see through the fog.

Suddenly, the fog seemed to part. A ship was in front of them. It was heading right for the *Martinez*!

"Hold on!" shouted the other passenger. Humphrey didn't have any time to think. He held on.

There was a loud noise as the ship hit the *Martinez*. People began shouting and crying.

Humphrey hurried to get his life preserver. People were running and pushing. They were racing about wildly and no one seemed to know what to do.

Men worked to put the life boats down. Some of the boats could not be put down into the sea. One boat, with children and women in it, seemed to be all right at first. Then it filled with water and turned over.

Humphrey was afraid. He could not swim. What should he do?

He ran down the steps to a lower deck. There, people were jumping into the water. He heard a cry behind him.

"The ship is going down! Jump! Swim for your lives!"

He jumped. The water was cold — so cold! The life preserver held him up. He could do nothing to help himself. He heard other passengers crying out. People from both ships were all around him in the water. He could not see them. He could only hear them.

As time passed, the fog closed in around him, and the cries for help grew fainter until there were no more. What had happened to all the other passengers? Would his journey end out here, alone in these cold waters?

Humphrey remembered all the bells and whistles he had heard. There were many ships close by. Surely, one would come and rescue him.

Suddenly, Humphrey spotted a ship coming slowly out of the fog. It came closer and closer. He reached out for it and then he looked up. He could see a man standing at the wheel. The man looked down and saw him in the water.

Humphrey heard shouts from above and a small boat was dropped into the water. They were coming to rescue him!

Out of the Fog

COMPREHENSION CHECK

Choose the best answer.

Preview Answer:
b. was on his way home.

1. When the fog rolled in, the *Martinez*
   ____a. sounded its whistle.
   ____b. slowed down.
   ____c. came to a stop.
   ____d. was in danger.

2. There was danger because
   ____a. it was getting dark.
   ____b. passing ships could not see one another.
   ____c. passing ships could not hear one another.
   ____d. ships' whistles would not work in the fog.

3. In order to stay clear of passing ships, the captain had to depend on his
   ____a. sense of direction.
   ____b. sense of smell.
   ____c. sense of hearing.
   ____d. passengers.

4. When the ship hit the *Martinez*, Humphrey hurried to get his
   ____a. clothes.
   ____b. money.
   ____c. life preserver.
   ____d. mother.

5. As the *Martinez* began to sink, some passengers were put into life boats, while others
   ____a. jumped into the sea.
   ____b. took swimming lessons.
   ____c. slept.
   ____d. laughed.

6. Humphrey
   ____a. was a good swimmer.
   ____b. did not know how to swim.
   ____c. was afraid of everything.
   ____d. was not afraid to drown.

7. Humphrey found the water to be
   ____a. very pleasant.
   ____b. very clean.
   ____c. very warm.
   ____d. very cold.

8. Humphrey was very sure that
   ____a. he was having a bad dream.
   ____b. he would drown.
   ____c. he would be rescued.
   ____d. he would be run over by a passing ship.

9. Another name for this story could be
   ____a. "Trouble at Sea."
   ____b. "Bells and Whistles."
   ____c. "Humphrey's Lonely Days at Sea."
   ____d. "Learning to Swim."

10. This story is mainly about
    ____a. how life preservers can save lives.
    ____b. how important it is to learn how to swim.
    ____c. Humphrey's journey at sea.
    ____d. Humphrey's rescue.

Check your answers with the key on page 67.

This page may be reproduced for classroom use.

Out of the Fog

VOCABULARY CHECK

deck	faint	fog	journey	passenger	rescue

I. Sentences to Finish

Fill in the blank in each sentence with the correct key word from the box above.

1. The_____smell of baked bread was coming from the kitchen.

2. The_____to Uncle Mike's house took us three days.

3. We went below_____to get out of the rain.

4. When driving through_____, it is important to keep your lights on.

5. I was the last_____to leave the airplane.

6. Joe climbed the tree to_____his cat.

II. Crossword Puzzle

Fill in the puzzle with the key words from the box above. Use the meanings below to help you choose the right word.

ACROSS
1. not loud; soft
2. save; take away from danger
3. a trip from one place to another

DOWN
1. someone on a boat, plane, train, car, or bus
2. the floor of a boat
3. a cloud near the ground

Check your answers with the key on page 69.

This page may be reproduced for classroom use.

The Cabin Boy

PREPARATION

Key Words

cabin	(ka´ bən)	a room in a ship *The passenger went to the <u>cabin</u> to get out of the rain.*
course	(kôrs)	a path from one place to another *The captain planned the ship's <u>course</u>.*
force	(fôrs)	to make a person act against his will *My mother always has to <u>force</u> me to clean my room.*
learn	(lėrn)	to find out something new *We will <u>learn</u> how to make ice cream at school* tomorrow.
lesson	(les´ n)	something to learn and remember *Tom has his skating <u>lesson</u> today.*
sailor	(sāl´ ər)	a worker on a ship; a person whose work is sailing *The <u>sailor</u> was painting the deck.*

The Cabin Boy

Necessary Words

died   (dīd)   stopped living
> *We were sad when our cat <u>died</u>.*

dying   (dī´ing)   about to die
> *Dad cut down the <u>dying</u> tree.*

dry   (drī)   not wet
> *His clothes were not <u>dry</u> enough to wear.*

gentleman   (jen´ tl mən)   a man who does not have to work for a living; a man of good family
> *The <u>gentleman</u> was sitting on the deck.*

hatch   (hach)   an opening in a ship's deck where freight is loaded
> *The captain opened the <u>hatch</u> and let the man come aboard.*

seal   (sēl)   a large, furry animal that lives in the sea
> *The <u>seal</u> was eating a fish.*

People

Cooky   is the ship's cook.

George Leach   is the *Ghost's* cabin boy.

Johansen   is a sailor aboard the *Ghost*.

Johnson   is a sailor aboard the *Ghost*.

Wolf Larsen   is the captain of the *Ghost*.

Things

Ghost   is the name of the ship that rescues Humphrey.

Lady Mine   is the name of a ship that passes the *Ghost*.

The Cabin Boy

Humphrey learns that he has been rescued by a seal-hunting boat.

Preview: 1. Read the name of the story.
2. Look at the picture.
3. Read the sentence under the picture.
4. Read the first four paragraphs of the story.
5. Then answer the following question.

You learned from your preview that when Humphrey was taken aboard the ship, he was

___a. warm, dry, and wide awake.
___b. tired, cold, and wet.
___c. not hungry.
___d. feeling very strong.

Turn to the Comprehension Check on page 16 for the right answer.

Now read the story.

Read to find out what Humphrey must do if he is to eat.

The Cabin Boy

Tired, cold, and very wet, Humphrey van Weyden lay on the deck. Two men stood over him.

"Feeling any better?" one asked. Together, they helped him sit up. One of them, Humphrey found out, was the cook, and the other was a sailor named Johnson. They gave him food to eat and something hot to drink.

The cook went away to get him some dry clothes.

"What ship is this?" Humphrey asked Johnson.

The sailor answered, "It's the *Ghost*, on course for waters where we'll soon be hunting seals."

The cook came back, bringing some of his own clothes. Humphrey put them on. They were dirty, and did not fit. But they were dry. The cook took the wet clothes to his cabin to dry them.

Humphrey saw the man who had spotted him in the water. "Who is that?" he asked.

"That's the captain, Wolf Larsen," said Johnson.

Wolf Larsen was watching a sailor who lay on his back on a hatch.

"It's the mate. He's dying," Johnson said. "The captain is very angry."

Humphrey watched. The man on the hatch rolled from side to side and a few minutes later, he died.

Wolf Larsen was talking to him. He called him terrible names. He walked up and down the deck, shouting wildly.

Suddenly, the captain stopped and looked at the cook. "Well, Cooky, that's the end of the mate," he said. "You must take really good care of yourself. We would not want anything to happen to you, would we?"

The cook seemed very frightened and hurried away.

Next, the captain turned to Humphrey.

"What work do you do?" the captain asked.

"I am a reader and a writer. I am a gentleman," Humphrey answered.

The captain took his hands and looked at them. "I can see you have never worked, for you have a lady's hands, soft and white."

"I have money," Humphrey said.

"Your father's money, I think. You live on money he worked for and left to you," said the captain. "You should learn what it is to work. I have an idea. Mr. Johansen will be the new mate. George Leach, the cabin boy, will be a sailor. You will be the cabin boy. Then I will have all the hands I need."

The cabin boy stepped up. "I don't wish to be a sailor. I signed on to be a cabin boy," he said with anger.

"Too bad," said the captain. He took a step toward George Leach and hit him. The cabin boy fell to the deck.

Humphrey was frightened, but he said, "You cannot force me to work on your ship. I want to go back to land."

The captain said, "First you have a lesson to learn about work. It is a lesson about what it is like to work for your food."

The fog had gone, and Humphrey saw a passing ship. "What is the name of that ship?" he asked.

"It's the *Lady Mine*," said Wolf Larsen.

"Change your course to meet it," Humphrey said. "I can go back home on the *Lady Mine*."

The captain only laughed.

Humphrey shouted as the ship got closer. "*Lady Mine*! This man is trying to force me to work for him. Come and rescue me and I will pay you well!"

A sailor shouted back, "Is something wrong over there?"

"Yes," Humphrey shouted, "I will pay you to take me with you!"

Wolf Larsen laughed again. "This one has had too much to drink!" he called to the sailor on the *Lady Mine*.

On the *Lady Mine*, the sailor waved, and the ship did not change course.

The captain watched it go. Then he turned to Humphrey and asked, "What is your name?"

"Humphrey van Weyden."

The captain said, "Humphrey van Weyden, go and find the cook and find out what your work will be."

15

The Cabin Boy

COMPREHENSION CHECK

Choose the best answer.

1. The *Ghost*
   _____a. is a small fishing boat.
   _____b. is a large seal-hunting ship.
   _____c. is a love boat.
   _____d. is a ship with many ghosts aboard.

2. The captain of the *Ghost* is
   _____a. Sea Wolf.
   _____b. Wolf Man.
   _____c. Wolf Johnson.
   _____d. Wolf Larsen.

3. Wolf Larsen
   _____a. was a friendly fellow.
   _____b. was a mean and terrible man.
   _____c. was loved by everyone.
   _____d. was a very old man.

4. The dying man aboard the ship was
   _____a. the mate.
   _____b. the cook.
   _____c. the cabin boy.
   _____d. the captain's brother.

5. When the mate died, Mr. Johansen became the new mate. What job did he give Humphrey van Weyden?
   _____a. The job of cook
   _____b. The job of captain
   _____c. The job of cabin boy
   _____d. The job of keeping the ship's watch

6. George Leach, who had been cabin boy, became angry when his job was given to Humphrey. When he told the captain that he did not wish to be a sailor, Wolf
   _____a. sent him home.
   _____b. threw him off the ship.
   _____c. hit him.
   _____d. sent him to his room.

7. Humphrey was frightened, but he told the captain that
   _____a. he would not work on his ship.
   _____b. he was going to teach him a lesson.
   _____c. he was a terrible captain.
   _____d. he would sink his ship if he was not taken back to land.

8. When Humphrey tried to get a passing ship to rescue him, Wolf Larsen tricked him by telling the men aboard that
   _____a. Humphrey was not in his right mind.
   _____b. Humphrey had had too much to drink.
   _____c. Humphrey was just having some fun.
   _____d. Humphrey was having a bad dream.

9. Another name for this story could be
   _____a. "Humphrey Gets a Job."
   _____b. "Rescued By a Wolf."
   _____c. "Hunting Seals."
   _____d. "A Man Dies at Sea."

10. This story is mainly about
    _____a. how to hunt for seals.
    _____b. a man who died at sea.
    _____c. a man who was rescued at sea.
    _____d. why Humphrey was afraid of Wolf Larsen.

Check your answers with the key on page 67.

This page may be reproduced for classroom use.

The Cabin Boy

VOCABULARY CHECK

cabin	course	force	learn	lesson	sailor

I. Sentences to Finish

Fill in the blank in each sentence with the correct key word from the box above.

1. It took the_____many days to paint his boat.

2. Because of the storm, the plane had to change its_____.

3. I had to_____the sick child to eat her soup.

4. The ship's captain kept a pet monkey in his_____.

5. My sister took her first swimming_____today.

6. Joe and I will_____how to skate today.

II. Word Search

All the words from the box above are hidden in the puzzle below. As you find each word, put a circle around it. One word, that is not a key word, has been done for you.

```
L E S S O N C A B
E C O U F S A I L
S A I L O R A B E
S C O U R S E L A
C A B E C A B I N
F O R L E A R N F
```

Check your answers with the key on page 69.

This page may be reproduced for classroom use.

Missing Money

PREPARATION

Key Words

expect	(eks pekt´)	to look for; what you think will happen *We expect to go to the circus today.*
fellow	(fel´ ō)	a man or boy *He was a tall fellow with red hair.*
lie	(lī)	something said that is not so *If he said he is my friend, it's a lie, because he isn't.*
neither	(nē´ ŦHər)	not one or the other *Neither of the boys can swim.*
pot	(pot)	a large pan for serving or cooking food *The pot was full of soup.*
reply	(ri plī´)	to answer *What will Sue reply when you ask her where she was?*

Missing Money

Necessary Words

galley   (gal´ ē)   a room on a ship where food is cooked
The cook fixed supper in the <u>galley</u>.

scold   (skōld)   to say angry words
Our mother will <u>scold</u> us for leaving our clothes on the floor.

spill   (spil)   to drop something so it falls all over
Be careful not to <u>spill</u> your milk.

staterooms   (stāt´ rümz)   rooms on a ship or train
Our <u>staterooms</u> were the biggest on the ship.

tea   (tē)   a drink made of water and the leaves of a plant
We had <u>tea</u> and bread for lunch.

Missing Money

Cooky makes Humphrey wash the pots.

Preview: 1. Read the name of the story.
2. Look at the picture.
3. Read the sentence under the picture.
4. Read the first four paragraphs of the story.
5. Then answer the following question.

You learned from your preview that Humphrey
___a. liked being the cabin boy.
___b. liked to wash pots.
___c. liked to tease Cooky.
___d. was afraid of the cook.

Turn to the Comprehension Check on page 22 for the right answer.

Now read the story.

Read to find out how Humphrey finds life aboard the *Ghost*.

Missing Money

Humphrey, the new cabin boy, set to work. He had to clean the cabin's four staterooms. The rest of the time, he worked for the cook. Cooky, Humphrey soon learned, was a mean little fellow. He liked to tease the new cabin boy.

Cooky watched as Humphrey washed one dirty pot after another.

"What a fine gentleman and what fine, clean lady's hands he has! Here's another pot to wash!" Cooky would say.

Humphrey wanted to reply, "Wash it yourself." But he was afraid — afraid of Cooky, and afraid of Wolf Larsen. He could stand up to neither of them. So he said nothing. He did his work.

A storm made life on the ship even harder. The wind blew and the *Ghost* rolled up and down on high waves.

Humphrey went out on deck with a pot of tea for the captain. He stepped through the galley door with it.

He heard a fellow call from above. "Here she comes! She's a big one!"

Then he heard the captain's voice. "Watch out, Hump —"

And he looked up to see a wave coming down on him.

A wall of water hit him. It threw him down and rolled him over and over. He was washed across the deck. When it was all over, he was sick with pain. His leg had been hurt.

The other sailors heard the captain call "Hump" to him, and soon they were all calling him Hump. None of them cared about his leg.

Cooky was angry that Hump spilled the tea. "What are you good for anyway? Can't even carry a bit of tea without losing it. Hurt your leg, I see — too bad. I expect you to do your work, Hump, same as ever," said Cooky.

Humphrey found his clothes. He was happy to have something clean to wear. He looked through them for his money, but it was gone.

"I had some money," Humphrey said to Cooky. "Where is it? You took it!"

"I didn't take it," Cooky replied. "That's a lie. I don't want to hear no more about it! And don't you be taking your lies to the captain."

Humphrey got a surprise when he went to clean Wolf Larsen's stateroom. The captain was a reader. He had books that Humphrey himself read and loved.

Later, he saw the captain alone on deck. He told him about the money.

"What did you expect?" the captain said. "You left your money in your clothes. So Cooky took it. This is a lesson for you. Learn to take care of your money yourself."

Humphrey could see then that the captain would not help him.

"That's wrong!" Humphrey replied. "You shouldn't let the fellow —"

"Keep something that isn't his? Isn't that what you have done all your life? Other people have made your food and your clothes. You have never worked for what you have. Neither you or Cooky have anything to be proud of. All people are pigs. They will take what they can, even if it isn't theirs."

The captain turned to leave, then he asked, "By the way, how much money did Cooky get?"

Humphrey told him, and the captain left.

Missing Money

COMPREHENSION CHECK

Choose the best answer.

1. Humphrey
   ____a. liked his new job as cabin boy.
   ____b. did not like his new job.
   ____c. was afraid to do his new job.
   ____d. was good at washing pots.

2. Why was Humphrey afraid of Wolf Larsen and the cook?
   ____a. They were stronger than he was.
   ____b. Wolf and Cooky carried guns.
   ____c. Wolf and Cooky carried big knives.
   ____d. Wolf Larsen and the cook were not in their right minds.

3. What did Humphrey drop when a big wave came down on him?
   ____a. The captain's dinner
   ____b. Cooky's dinner
   ____c. The captain's pot of tea
   ____d. Cooky's tea

4. The wave that washed Humphrey across the deck left him with pain
   ____a. in his knee.
   ____b. in his arm.
   ____c. in his leg.
   ____d. in his foot.

5. No one aboard the *Ghost* seemed to care
   ____a. how hard Humphrey worked.
   ____b. that Cooky was lazy.
   ____c. about Humphrey's new job.
   ____d. about Humphrey's bad leg.

6. Cooky was angry that Hump
   ____a. was a cry-baby.
   ____b. spilled the tea.
   ____c. was a good cabin boy.
   ____d. hurt his leg.

7. What made Humphrey think that Cooky had taken his money?
   ____a. Cooky was a known thief.
   ____b. Humphrey's money had been in the clothes that Cooky had put out to dry.
   ____c. He found Cooky counting money.
   ____d. Someone told Humphrey that Cooky had taken it.

8. When Humphrey told the captain that Cooky had taken his money, Wolf Larsen
   ____a. laughed at Humphrey.
   ____b. beat up the cook.
   ____c. had Cooky give the money back.
   ____d. would not help Humphrey.

9. Another name for this story could be
   ____a. "Humphrey Learns a Lesson."
   ____b. "Another Pot to Wash!"
   ____c. "Clean Clothes for Humphrey."
   ____d. "Humphrey Hurts his Leg."

10. This story is mainly about
   ____a. a man who hurts his leg at sea.
   ____b. a man who learns that life at sea will not be pleasant.
   ____c. how Humphrey learns to take care of himself.
   ____d. how hard Humphrey works for Cooky.

Check your answers with the key on page 67.

This page may be reproduced for classroom use.

Missing Money

VOCABULARY CHECK

expect	fellow	lie	neither	pot	reply

I. Sentences to Finish

Fill in the blank in each sentence with the correct key word from the box above.

1. We cooked popcorn in a_____over the stove.

2. When I ask someone a question I_____them to answer me.

3. When Jim asked Sue for a date, she didn't know how to_____.

4. The young_____next door is a good friend of mine.

5. Walter told a_____when he said he was in school today.

6. Both girls were sad because_____of them were asked to dance.

II. Matching

Write the letter of the correct meaning from Column B next to the key word in Column A.

Column A	Column B
_____1. neither	a. to answer
_____2. reply	b. a man or a boy
_____3. pot	c. to look for; what you think will happen
_____4. lie	d. a large pan
_____5. expect	e. something said that is not so
_____6. fellow	f. not one or the other

Check your answers with the key on page 69.

This page may be reproduced for classroom use.

Cooky

PREPARATION

Key Words

drank	(drangk)	took in water, milk, etc. *I drank a whole can of pop.*
knife	(nīf)	a tool used for cutting *She took the knife and cut the cake.*
repeat	(ri pēt´)	to say again *Would you repeat what you just said?*
sharp	(shärp)	having a thin cutting edge or a fine point *The knife was so sharp that I cut myself.*
strike	(strīk)	to give a blow to; to hit *The Army waited until dark to strike the camp.*
wouldn't	(wüd´ nt)	would not *The baby wouldn't wear her shoes.*

Cooky

Necessary Words

job   (job)   work that is done every day
Mary has a <u>job</u> at a store.

pour   (pôr)   to move a liquid from one place to another
Please <u>pour</u> me a glass of milk.

shake   (shāk)   to hold and move back and forth or up and down
Jill went over to <u>shake</u> the new girl's hand.

swabs   (swobz)   another name for sailors
The <u>swabs</u> were busy washing the deck.

whiskey (hwis' kē)   a strong drink made from grain
Bob drank too much <u>whiskey</u> at the party.

Cooky

*Wolf Larsen and Humphrey talked for many hours.
Humphrey liked being around the captain.*

Preview: 1. Read the name of the story.
               2. Look at the picture.
               3. Read the sentences under the picture.
               4. Read the first paragraph of the story.
               5. Then answer the following question.

You learned from your preview that

___a. Wolf Larsen didn't know right from wrong.
___b. Wolf Larsen knew nothing about life.
___c. Humphrey was not getting any rest.
___d. Humphrey's leg was getting better.

Turn to the Comprehension Check on page 28 for the right answer.

Now read the story.

Read to find out how Humphrey stands up to Cooky.

Cooky

Humphrey had many talks with Wolf Larsen. They talked about books and about life. They talked about right and wrong. Humphrey liked their talks and he also liked being around the captain. He didn't have to work for Cooky while he was talking to Wolf. With rest, his leg was slowly getting better.

One day after dinner, the captain called Cooky to his stateroom. He had Humphrey bring a bottle of whiskey and two glasses and he poured drinks. Cooky drank his quickly. The captain poured him more.

"Now then, Cooky," said the captain. "Let's play cards."

They played for money. They drank whiskey and played cards for hours. The captain won. Over and over, he won every game they played. Cooky lost all his money.

"Cooky needs some air," Wolf Larsen said. "Take him up on deck, Humphrey."

Cooky had had too much whiskey. He could hardly walk. Humphrey took him up on deck and left him. The captain had told Leach to pour water on him. Humphrey heard Cooky shout as the cold water hit him.

Humphrey went back to see the captain. Wolf was counting his winnings.

"What you have won belongs to me," Humphrey said.

"It belongs to me, now," said the captain.

"But —" began Humphrey.

"Must I repeat it?" the captain asked. "It's my money now, so you just go away."

That was not the end of it. Now, Cooky was angry at Humphrey. Humphrey had not worked for days, and Cooky was forced to do the hard work himself. Cooky lost all his money in the card game, while Humphrey watched. Cooky wouldn't rest until he made Humphrey pay.

The galley had one sharp knife. Cooky began to sharpen it on a stone. He looked up at Humphrey, then at the knife.

The sailors whispered, "He's getting ready to strike. Humphrey is in for it."

Before that could happen, the cook went after Leach. He was angry because Leach had poured water on him. He cut Leach's arm in a fight.

And he kept on sharpening.

Humphrey went to the captain for help.

"Kill him, and I'll give you his job," Wolf Larsen said.

So Humphrey was on his own. He had to do something, or Cooky would hurt him or kill him. He took some cans of milk from the galley and gave them to a seal hunter for his knife.

The next morning, Cooky sharpened his knife. He was talking to a sailor.

Cooky said, "Yes, I cut him bad! He was hurt, but didn't I go on and strike again? I cut him to the bone."

Cooky looked up at Humphrey. He repeated, "Yes, I cut him bad."

Humphrey sat down and began to sharpen *his* new knife. Both men sat there, not saying anything. They sharpened and sharpened. Soon everyone on the ship was in the galley, hoping to see the fight.

Two hours passed, and then the cook stood up. He put his knife down and he said, "Humphrey, you're all right. I likes you, in a way, and I'll be happy to shake your hand."

Cooky had backed down because he was afraid to fight. Humphrey saw that there was nothing to be frightened of. He, Hump, the cabin boy, had won. Humphrey wouldn't put his hand out.

"All right, take it or leave it," said Cooky. "Get out, you swabs!" he shouted at the sailors.

Cooky

COMPREHENSION CHECK

Choose the best answer.

1. Humphrey liked spending time with the captain because
   _____a. he found him interesting.
   _____b. it made Cooky angry.
   _____c. the captain gave him whiskey.
   _____d. the captain seemed to know everything.

2. Why did Wolf Larsen want to play cards with Cooky?
   _____a. No one else would play with him.
   _____b. Humphrey didn't know how to play cards.
   _____c. He wanted to win back Humphrey's money.
   _____d. He wanted to show Humphrey how well he played cards.

3. Wolf Larsen
   _____a. won three out of four games.
   _____b. won every game.
   _____c. got tired of playing and gave up.
   _____d. lost all his money.

4. Wolf Larsen probably won because
   _____a. Cooky was not a good card player.
   _____b. Cooky had been working so hard that he was tired.
   _____c. Cooky let him win.
   _____d. Cooky had been drinking too much whiskey.

5. Humphrey asked Wolf Larsen
   _____a. if he would teach him how to play cards.
   _____b. for his money back.
   _____c. for the night off.
   _____d. how much money he had won.

6. Why did Cooky have it in for Humphrey?
   _____a. He didn't like his looks.
   _____b. Humphrey had laughed at him.
   _____c. Humphrey had poured cold water on him.
   _____d. While Humphrey had spent time with the captain, Cooky was forced to do Hump's work.

7. When Humphrey told the captain that Cooky had it in for him, Wolf Larsen told him
   _____a. to kill Cooky.
   _____b. that Cooky would get over his anger.
   _____c. not to worry.
   _____d. that he would talk to Cooky.

8. Humphrey frightened Cooky by
   _____a. cleaning his gun.
   _____b. sharpening his own knife.
   _____c. making friends with the men on ship.
   _____d. being friendly.

9. Another name for this story could be
   _____a. "Shaking Hands."
   _____b. "The Card Game."
   _____c. "Humphrey's 'Win'."
   _____d. "Wolf Counts his Money."

10. This story is mainly about
    _____a. a man who learns to stand up for himself.
    _____b. a cook that drinks too much.
    _____c. a captain who likes to play cards.
    _____d. how to sharpen a knife.

Check your answers with the key on page 67.

This page may be reproduced for classroom use.

Cooky

VOCABULARY CHECK

drank	knife	repeat	sharp	strike	wouldn't

I. Sentences to Finish
Fill in the blank in each sentence with the correct key word from the box above.

1. Phil_____so much pop that he could not eat his dinner.

2. I_____do that if I were you.

3. My pencil has a very_____point.

4. "I can't hear you. Will you_____that?"

5. Harold has lost his good hunting_____.

6. When someone hits you, be ready to_____back.

II. Using The Words
On the lines below, write six of your own sentences using the key words from the box above. Use each word once, drawing a line under the key word.

1. _____

2. _____

3. _____

4. _____

5. _____

6. _____

Check your answers with the key on page 70.

This page may be reproduced for classroom use.

The New Mate

PREPARATION

Key Words

bunk	(bunk)	a bed on a ship; a narrow bed set against a wall like a shelf *The sailor was asleep in his <u>bunk</u>.*
ocean	(ō´ shən)	a large body of salt water; a sea *Fish swim in the <u>ocean</u>.*
search	(sėrch)	to look for *The children began to <u>search</u> for their lost dog.*
shape	(shāp)	form *Tonya saw a dark <u>shape</u> moving across the water.*
slept	(slept)	had been sleeping *He <u>slept</u> until morning.*
you've	(yüv)	you have *I think <u>you've</u> done a good job.*

The New Mate

Necessary Words

beat	(bēt)	to hit someone with one's hands and fists *The captain would <u>beat</u> the men when they didn't do what he said.*
murderer	(mėr´ dər ər)	one who kills another *The <u>murderer</u> killed two people.*
oilskins	(oil´ skinz)	a sailor's suit, used to keep out the cold and water *The sailors all had <u>oilskins</u> for times when there were storms.*
worthless	(wėrth´ lis)	of no value or worth *The broken car was <u>worthless</u> to anyone.*

The New Mate

Humphrey could do nothing to stop the terrible beating.

> ***Preview:***
> 1. Read the name of the story.
> 2. Look at the picture.
> 3. Read the sentence under the picture.
> 4. Read the first two paragraphs of the story.
> 5. Then answer the following question.
>
> You learned from your preview that Johnson was beaten by
> ___a. Wolf Larsen.
> ___b. Cooky.
> ___c. Wolf Larsen and Johansen.
> ___d. Humphrey van Weyden.
>
> *Turn to the Comprehension Check on page 34 for the right answer.*

Now read the story.

Read to find out who becomes the new mate aboard the *Ghost*.

The New Mate

It was a day of fights. The fights started because Cooky overheard Johnson talking about his oilskins. He had bought them from the ship's store. They were worthless, he said.

After Cooky told the captain, Wolf called Johnson to his stateroom. Together, he and Johansen beat Johnson. Humphrey was there to see the terrible beating. It went on until Johnson stopped moving.

When it was over, they threw him out on the deck.

George Leach, the old cabin boy, found Johnson. He helped him to his bunk and took care of him. Then he went to talk to Wolf Larsen.

Humphrey was there to hear everything.

"You've nearly killed Johnson. It was easy, wasn't it — two men beating one? You are a murderer and a pig, Wolf Larsen. A pig! A pig! A pig!" George Leach said. He went on and on, calling the captain every terrible name he could think of.

Humphrey couldn't believe his ears. How could George Leach, only a boy, stand up to the captain?

Wolf just sat and listened. He seemed to like it. He watched George Leach like a cat watches a mouse.

That made the boy even more angry. He wouldn't stop.

"Come and kill me, you pig!" he shouted. "You murderer — I'm not afraid of you!"

Cooky said, "My, my, such bad words!"

At that, Leach turned on Cooky and beat him. It was a beating every bit as bad as the one the captain and Johansen had given Johnson. No one tried to help Cooky, just as no one had tried to help Johnson.

Later that day, the seal hunters began to fight with each other. Humphrey wondered how it would all end. The answer wasn't long in coming.

One night three days later, Humphrey was on the deck. He saw a dark shape climb out of the ocean. It came up over the side of the ship. It was the captain.

"Help me search for the mate, Hump," spoke the captain. "Help me find Johansen. I think we may have lost him overboard."

Humphrey followed the captain. Why had Wolf and Johansen been in the ocean? Humphrey wondered whether they fell in, or had been pushed.

They searched for Johansen along the decks. He was not there. Next, they went down to where the sailors slept. There were twelve bunks. Eight sailors slept in their bunks. Wolf hoped that he would find Johansen there.

The captain looked at each one carefully. Humphrey followed with a light. They got to Leach's and Johnson's bunks.

Something moved quickly. Humphrey's light was knocked out of his hand. Humphrey could see nothing, but he could hear what was happening. Leach and Johnson were beating the captain.

"Get a knife!" Leach shouted. "We'll kill him!"

The other sailors woke up and wanted to know who was being beaten. They couldn't see the captain because he was only a shape in the dark.

"It's Johansen! Leach lied.

The sailors hated Johansen. Seven of them piled on and began beating the captain, but he was able to force his way out.

He was badly hurt, so Humphrey helped him back to his stateroom and took care of him.

"Well done, Hump," Wolf Larsen said. "As you know, with Johansen gone, we'll need a mate. So from now on, you're the mate."

Humphrey said, "No, not me, I don't need a new job."

A hard look came into the captain's eye and he replied, "Good night, Mr. van Weyden."

The New Mate

COMPREHENSION CHECK

Choose the best answer.

1. Why was Johnson beaten up?
    _____a. Johnson had taken some milk from the ship's store.
    _____b. Johnson had taken money from the ship's store.
    _____c. Johnson said the ship's store had sold him worthless goods.
    _____d. Johnson was beaten for using bad language.

2. Why didn't Humphrey try to help Johnson?
    _____a. He believed that Johnson deserved the beating.
    _____b. He knew that Johnson didn't want his help.
    _____c. He thought that Johnson could win the fight without him.
    _____d. He was afraid he would be beaten too.

3. Who found Johnson and helped him to his bunk?
    _____a. Johansen
    _____b. Cooky
    _____c. George Leach
    _____d. Wolf

4. Angry that Johnson had been beaten, George Leach went to the captain. He called him
    _____a. every terrrible name he could think of.
    _____b. a fat pig.
    _____c. a dirty dog.
    _____d. a mean killer.

5. Goerge Leach
    _____a. was afraid of what the captain would do to him.
    _____b. was not afraid of Wolf Larsen.
    _____c. was a murderer.
    _____d. was a pig.

6. Who do you think threw Wolf Larsen and Johansen overboard?
    _____a. Cooky
    _____b. Hump
    _____c. Several of the hunters on board
    _____d. Leach and Johnson

7. Leach and Johnson were trying to
    _____a. kill the captain.
    _____b. please the captain.
    _____c. make the captain angry.
    _____d. frighten the captain.

8. What do you suppose happened to Johansen?
    _____a. He was sleeping in someone else's stateroom.
    _____b. He had escaped on one of the small boats aboard the *Ghost*.
    _____c. He was playing a game of "Cat and Mouse."
    _____d. He had drowned.

9. Another name for this story could be
    _____a. "Murder at Sea."
    _____b. "Ocean Breezes."
    _____c. "Humphrey's New Job."
    _____d. "Standing Up to the Captain."

10. This story is mainly about
    _____a. the terrible things that happened aboard the *Ghost*.
    _____b. a captain who was loved.
    _____c. Humphrey's new job.
    _____d. how Leach cared for Johnson after the fight.

Check your answers with the key on page 67.

The New Mate

VOCABULARY CHECK

bunk	ocean	search	shape	slept	you've

I. Sentences to Finish

Fill in the blank in each sentence with the correct key word from the box above.

1. "_____ really done it this time Hank!"

2. An apple is different in_____from a banana.

3. Our family went_____fishing last week-end.

4. My best friend, Jill_____over last Saturday.

5. At camp last year, I slept in the bottom_____.

6. We went to the beach in_____of shells.

II. Put an X next to the best ending for each sentence.

1. If <u>you've</u> had a bad cold,
   ___a. it means your brother was sick.
   ___b. it means that you were sick.

2. A <u>bunk</u>
   ___a. is found on your foot.
   ___b. is a narrow bed.

3. If you have <u>slept</u>,
   ___a. it means that you're tired.
   ___b. it means that you're well-rested.

4. The <u>ocean</u>
   ___a. is a large body of sweet water.
   ___b. is a sea.

5. The <u>shape</u> of an apple
   ___a. is red.
   ___b. is round.

6. To <u>search</u>
   ___a. means to find something.
   ___b. means to look for something.

Check your answers with the key on page 70.

This page may be reproduced for classroom use.

The Hunt

PREPARATION

Key Words

coffee   (kôf´ē)   a drink made from the beans of a plant
The men drank <u>coffee</u> from white cups.

curl   (kėrl)   a curve or twist
Each ocean wave has a <u>curl</u> as it reaches land.

sail   (sāl)   a large cloth sheet spread to the wind to make a ship move through the water
The ship's <u>sail</u> was wet with rain.

slide   (slīd)   to move smoothly as a sled moves on snow or ice
We saw the boat <u>slide</u> over the wave.

spray   (sprā)   a liquid going through the air in fine drops
The ocean <u>spray</u> made the deck wet.

tumble   (tum´ bl)   to fall
Bill began to <u>tumble</u> off the ladder.

The Hunt

Necessary Words

hated	(hā´ t´əd)	disliked greatly *Humphrey <u>hated</u> the cook.*
jib	(jib)	one of a ship's sails *The <u>jib</u> was lost during the storm.*
masts	(masts)	tall wood posts that hold a ship's sails *The ship had two <u>masts</u>.*
rigging	(rig´ ging)	the wires and ropes used to control a ship's sails *The boy climbed up the ship's <u>rigging</u> to fix the broken mast.*

The Hunt

A sudden storm puts the hunters' lives in great danger.

Preview: 1. Read the name of the story.
                      2. Look at the picture.
                      3. Read the sentence under the picture.
                      4. Read the first four paragraphs of the story.
                      5. Then answer the following question.

You learned from your preview that

___a. Humphrey's life was better.

___b. Humphrey's life was worse than ever.

___c. Humphrey's life was coming to an end.

___d. Humphrey was working harder these days.

Turn to the Comprehension Check on page 40 for the right answer.

Now read the story.

Read to find out what happens to the hunters and their boats.

The Hunt

Humphrey's life was better. He had gotten away from Cooky and no longer had to work so hard. He learned the mate's job, and he did it well.

Everyone called him Mr. van Weyden now.

Still, all was not well. The sailors had tried to kill the captain and he was making them pay for it.

There were more beatings and fights. The captain picked on Johnson and Leach the most.

Johnson was frightened. He told Humphrey he expected the captain to kill him.

Leach was angry. He hated the captain and he would have killed him, if he could have. Wolf Larsen was too clever for that.

"Why don't you just kill Leach and be done with it?" Humphrey asked the captain. "It would be kinder."

"You're wrong," said the captain. "Leach is really alive for the first time in his life! He hopes to kill me. That's all he lives for. It's all he thinks about. This is wonderful for him!"

The fights and beatings stopped when the hunt started. The hunters went out in boats. They killed seals and cut off their skins. It went on day after day. The skins piled up on the deck.

One day, a storm came up suddenly. The hunting boats were at sea, far across the water.

"We must go after them," the captain said. "You men — put that sail up!"

A cold wind began blowing. The ship, its sails filling with wind, raced across the ocean. Humphrey and the captain searched the waters, looking for the missing boats.

The wind blew harder yet and the waves began to curl higher. Spray filled the air and the ocean washed the Ghost's decks.

The sailors worked terribly hard. Even Cooky worked, making pots of coffee. It warmed the men and kept them going.

At last, a hunting boat was spotted. It rolled up over the top of a wave. Humphrey watched it slide down the other side.

"We must change course," the captain said. "Mr. van Weyden! Make ready to back the jib."

Humphrey was not ready. Huge waves were hitting the ship. Spray washed over him. The wind knocked him down. One wave curled over, hitting him hard. He began to tumble across the deck. He jumped up and ran to fix the jib. If he didn't do it, the ship would go over!

Humphrey stood against the wind and pulled on the jib. At last, the job was done. He looked up and saw a hunting boat. There were three hunters in it. It was only about 20 feet away! It was tumbling across the ocean toward the Ghost.

It came sliding up over a wave. The wave came up even with the deck. The three hunters jumped across to the Ghost. With the next wave, the sailors pulled the boat onto the deck.

"Now, Mr. van Weyden, climb..." the captain shouted, "and look for more boats!"

Humphrey quickly climbed the rigging. He held on, looking out at the huge waves washing over the ship. The masts seemed to come right up out of the ocean. He couldn't see the Ghost's decks at all.

About an hour later, he spotted another boat. It was bottom up, with three men hanging on.

The men were soon rescued. The boat was broken in many places, but the sailors pulled it onto the ship.

They kept searching for the other boats. Night came and it was too dark to see, so they gave up looking. Everyone went to the cabin for more coffee and some food. Humphrey ate and drank his fill.

"How many men will they lose in this storm?" thought Humphrey. "How many will be hurt?" he asked himself. Humphrey felt he had been lucky.

39

The Hunt

COMPREHENSION CHECK

Choose the best answer.

1. Why was everyone calling Humphrey Mr. van Weyden now?
   _____a. The captain ordered them to.
   _____b. They were trying to please him because he was the captain's friend.
   _____c. They were teasing him.
   _____d. Because Humphrey was doing a great job as the new mate.

2. The sailors couldn't kill Wolf Larsen because
   _____a. the captain killed them first.
   _____b. the captain was too clever.
   _____c. the sailors were not lucky men.
   _____d. the sailors were tired and hungry.

3. Who did the captain pick on the most?
   _____a. Leach and Johnson
   _____b. Leach and Cooky
   _____c. Humphrey and Cooky
   _____d. Leach and Humphrey

4. The hunters went out in boats to hunt for
   _____a. sheep.
   _____b. squirrels.
   _____c. seals.
   _____d. silver.

5. The seals were hunted
   _____a. for fun.
   _____b. for their skins.
   _____c. for their tasty meat.
   _____d. to please Wolf Larsen.

6. When a storm came up suddenly, the hunters
   _____a. kept right on hunting for seals.
   _____b. headed for dry land.
   _____c. headed for home.
   _____d. were in danger of drowning.

7. The men aboard the *Ghost*
   _____a. searched all night for the missing men.
   _____b. searched for the men for about one hour.
   _____c. searched for the men until it became too dark to see.
   _____d. searched until they found all the men.

8. How many missing boats were found and rescued?
   _____a. Two
   _____b. Three
   _____c. Four
   _____d. All of them

9. Another name for this story could be
   _____a. "The Search."
   _____b. "A Clever Captain."
   _____c. "Humphrey's Luck."
   _____d. "A job Well Done."

10. This story is mainly about
   _____a. how well Humphrey learned the mate's job.
   _____b. why Leach wanted to kill the captain.
   _____c. the hard life of a seal hunter.
   _____d. how some men at sea came to be in danger.

Check your answers with the key on page 67.

This page may be reproduced for classroom use.

The Hunt

VOCABULARY CHECK

coffee	curl	sail	slide	spray	tumble

I. Sentences to Finish

Fill in the blank in each sentence with the correct key word from the box above.

1. I watched the skaters_____easily across the ice.

2. The wind ripped our main_____and we had to fix it.

3. She uses hair_____to keep her hair in place.

4. Dad drinks three cups of_____with breakfast.

5. I watched the young boy_____off his bike.

6. Mother will_____my hair for the party.

II. Matching

Unscramble the groups of letters to spell out the key words. Match the key words in Column A with their meanings in Column B.

COLUMN A

elids   1. _____

blumet   2. _____

effoce   3. _____

clur   4. _____

prays   5. _____

ails   6. _____

COLUMN B

a. a curve or twist

b. a large cloth sheet that makes a ship move through the water

c. to move smoothly as a sled moves on snow or ice

d. a liquid going through the air in fine drops

e. a drink made from the beans of a plant

f. to fall

Check your answers with the key on page 70.

This page may be reproduced for classroom use.

Lost

PREPARATION

Key Words

breeze	(brēz)	a light wind *A breeze lifted the flag.*
sank	(sangk)	fell to the bottom *The ship sank in the water.*
steer	(stēr)	to set on the course wanted; to guide *The captain took the wheel to steer the ship.*
trap	trap)	a way to catch someone or something *Mr. Brown set a trap to catch the rabbit.*
weather	(weŦH´ər)	conditions outside — rain, snow, etc. *If the weather is warm, we will swim.*
welcome	(wel´ kəm)	to greet; to say hello to *John went to the door to welcome his friends.*

Lost

Necessary Words

hundred   (hun´ dred)   100

> *There were more than four <u>hundred</u> people at the game.*

mend   (mend)   to fix; repair

> *The sailors were told to <u>mend</u> the broken boat.*

raged   (rājd)   became very angry

> *The captain <u>raged</u> at Leach and Johnson.*

Places

Japan   a country, east of Asia, made up of islands

Lost

As the Ghost sets out to find Johnson and Leach, they spot another boat. But it isn't one of their own. Four men and a young woman are taken aboard.

Preview: 1. Read the name of the story.
2. Look at the picture.
3. Read the sentences under the picture.
4. Read the first two paragraphs of the story.
5. Then answer the following question.

You learned from your preview that the storm took the lives of

___a. three men.
___b. thirty men.
___c. four men.
___d. fourteen men.

Turn to the Comprehension Check on page 46 for the right answer.

Now read the story.

Read to find out what becomes of Johnson and Leach.

Lost

Slowly, the storm blew itself out. As the weather got better, the *Ghost* went on searching for the missing.

Other ships had picked up two of the *Ghost's* boats and rescued some of her men. In all, only four men were lost. The sailors mended the boats and the seal hunt started again.

Asked to steer the ship, Humphrey took the wheel for hours at a time. One afternoon, Leach came to him with a question.

"How far are we from Japan?"

"About five hundred miles," answered Humphrey.

The next morning, Johnson and Leach were gone. They had taken a boat. They had taken water and food, too.

When he found out, Wolf Larsen raged. They wouldn't get away with it! He set off to look for them.

Two days later, a boat was spotted. It wasn't Johnson and Leach. There were five people in it.

As the boat got closer, one of the sailors said, "Oh, my. Here's trouble!"

"What do you mean?" Humphrey asked.

"One of them's a woman!" said the sailor.

"Welcome her, Mr. van Weyden," said the captain. "Show her to a cabin."

Four men and a woman were taken off the boat.

The woman was young. She was very tired. Humphrey took her to the cabin to rest.

She knew they were close to Japan. She said, "We are not far from land, are we? We could be there tonight."

Humphrey replied, "Our captain is a strange man, and you can't be sure of anything with him."

Humphrey left the woman asleep in the cabin. He went out on deck to find that the *Ghost* had come across another boat. This time, it *was* Johnson and Leach.

"Good thing," said a sailor, "for you can feel from that breeze that the weather won't hold for long. There's a storm coming and they would never have made it to land."

"Did you welcome the lady?" the captain asked Humphrey.

"Yes. She's asleep," Humphrey said. "What will you do with Johnson and Leach?" he asked.

"I won't kill them," the captain answered.

The *Ghost* was leaving the boat behind. Humphrey expected the captain to turn the ship. The man who was steering did not change course.

The breeze had become a wind. The little boat was

taking on water. It raced after the *Ghost*, trying to catch up with her.

Suddenly, the captain turned the ship around. Johnson's and Leach's boat got closer. The *Ghost* turned around once more.

And so it went. Again and again the ship went away, then turned around. The little boat with the two men in it could never catch up with her. Humphrey began to see what was happening. It was a trap! The *Ghost* was leading the boat into the storm.

Rain began falling as the wind blew harder and harder. Waves hit the little boat, filling it with water until it sank into the tumbling water. The trap had worked. Johnson and Leach sank as the other men watched.

Smiling, the captain changed course again—away from Japan! They were going back to hunt for seals.

One of the rescued men had watched as the captain had laid his trap for Johnson and Leach.

"What kind of ship *is* this?" he asked Humphrey.

"You have eyes—you've seen what it is," Humphrey replied.

Lost

COMPREHENSION CHECK

Choose the best answer.

1. Johnson and Leach had taken one of the small boats and set out for
   _____a. China.
   _____b. Japan.
   _____c. Africa.
   _____d. home.

2. When Wolf Larsen learned that Johnson and Leach had taken off in one of the boats,
   _____a. he set off to look for them.
   _____b. he didn't bother to look for them.
   _____c. he was sad that they had left.
   _____d. he was pleased that they were gone.

3. When the captain spotted Johnson and Leach,
   _____a. he brought them aboard and beat them.
   _____b. he brought them aboard and killed them.
   _____c. he sank their boat.
   _____d. he left them behind.

4. Each time Johnson and Leach tried to catch up with the *Ghost*,
   _____a. Wolf Larsen turned the boat around, and sailed away from them.
   _____b. the wind blew harder, and they couldn't catch up to the ship.
   _____c. rain would fill their boat, causing them to slow down.
   _____d. the waves would take them farther out to sea.

5. Wolf Larsen was setting a trap for Johnson and Leach that would
   _____a. teach them a lesson.
   _____b. make them sorry that they had run away.
   _____c. lead them into the storm.
   _____d. lead them to a safe place.

6. What became of Johnson and Leach?
   _____a. They swam to Japan.
   _____b. They were rescued by another boat.
   _____c. They were run over by a passing ship.
   _____d. They drowned.

7. Wolf Larsen
   _____a. was pleased that his trap had worked.
   _____b. felt bad for what he had done.
   _____c. missed Johnson and Leach.
   _____d. was getting tired of his life at sea.

8. The men aboard the *Ghost* did nothing to help Johnson and Leach because
   _____a. no one liked the two men.
   _____b. they didn't know how to help them.
   _____c. they feared the captain would kill them too.
   _____d. they were too busy doing their own work.

9. Another name for this story could be
   _____a. "A Deadly Trap."
   _____b. "500 Miles From Japan."
   _____c. "The Lady Aboard the *Ghost*."
   _____d. "Wolf Larsen's Rage."

10. This story is mainly about
    _____a. how Wolf Larsen got even with Johnson and Leach.
    _____b. how Humphrey learned to steer the ship.
    _____c. a lovely young woman who came aboard the *Ghost*.
    _____d. seal hunting in bad weather.

Check your answers with the key on page 67.

This page may be reproduced for classroom use.

Lost

VOCABULARY CHECK

breeze	sank	steer	trap	weather	welcome

I. Sentences to Finish

Fill in the blank in each sentence with the correct key word from the box above.

1. The cool night_____felt good after the hot day we had.

2. The_____calls for light rain today.

3. Mr. Winter's boat_____during the storm.

4. Mother says my friends are always_____in our home.

5. Martha was careful to_____the sled around the tree.

6. Dad set a_____to catch the tricky rabbit.

II. Word Search

Find the key words in the puzzle below. They may be written from left to right, from top to botton, or on an angle. Circle each word you find. One word, that is not a key word, has been done for you.

```
K   S   T   E   E   P   S   A   N   D
I   B   R   O   W   G   A   R   J   A
W   S   A   W   E   L   L   M   B   B
S   T   P   E   E   X   E   D   R   W
A   E   X   L   S   A   N   K   E   E
V   E   U   C   Q   Z   T   T   E   L
I   R   N   O   C   H   O   H   Z   C
X   W   E   M   L   B   R   E   E   Q
R   Q   S   E   P  (T   R   E   E)  R
```

Check your answers with the key on page 71.

This page may be reproduced for classroom use.

MAUD

PREPARATION

Key Words

certainly   (sėrt´ n lē)   surely
> We <u>certainly</u> have been having good weather.

gentle   (jen´ tl)   kind; not rough
> The teacher was a <u>gentle</u> and good woman.

happiness   (hap´ ē nis)   well-being; joy
> Humphrey was filled with <u>happiness</u> at the thought of going home.

joy   (joi)   happiness; pleasure; delight
> Tim shouted with <u>joy</u> when he saw the birthday cake.

respect   (ri spekt´)   to think highly of
> Beth was brave, which made people <u>respect</u> her.

wrote   (rōt)   put words on paper
> Mr. Dane <u>wrote</u> books about dogs.

MAUD

Necessary Words

argue(d)   (är´ gū)   to speak against or for
> *Jack will often <u>argue</u> with his mother about walking the dog.*

earn   (ėrn)   to work to get
> *Missy hopes to <u>earn</u> money for a new bike.*

fade (faded)   (fād)   to go away
> *At first the sound was loud, then it <u>faded</u>.*

meal   (mēl)   food that is eaten at a certain time, such as breakfast
> *Our biggest <u>meal</u> was at noon.*

newspaper   (nüz´ pā´ pər)   a printed record of the day's news, weather, and sports
> *Every morning, I read the <u>newspaper</u> a while.*

People

Death Larsen   is Wolf Larsen's brother. He is the captain of a seal-hunting ship, too.

Maud Brewster   is a young woman rescued by the *Ghost*.

Things

Macedonia   is the name of Death Larsen's ship.

MAUD

Smiling, Maud asks the captain, "When will we reach Japan?"

Preview: 1. Read the name of the story.
2. Look at the picture.
3. Read the sentence under the picture.
4. Read the first three paragraphs of the story.
5. Then answer the following question.

You learned from your preview that Humphrey thought Maud was

___a. too pretty to eat with the men.
___b. too gentle to eat with the men.
___c. too sick to eat with the men.
___d. too young to eat with the men.

Turn to the Comprehension Check on page 52 for the right answer.

Now read the story.

Read to find out how Maud Brewster surprises Humphrey.

MAUD

The four rescued men felt no joy. They certainly had not expected this! The captain was forcing them to work on the ship. They saw what happened to Leach and Johnson, so they would do what Wolf Larsen told them to do.

The woman's name was Maud Brewster. Humphrey wanted her meals brought to her cabin. She seemed too gentle to eat with the men. The captain had other ideas.

So they sat down to their first meal with her. "When will we reach Japan?" she asked the captain, smiling.

"In three or four months, if the hunt ends early," he replied.

Her happiness faded. She argued. Wolf would not listen.

"We can't stop the hunt just for you. We must work," he said. "Unlike you, we have to earn our food."

"I work," she said. "I am a writer."

Suddenly, Humphrey knew who this lady was. He was filled with joy. He had read Maud's book! He had written about it for the newspaper!

"I read your book. I wrote about your book!" he cried.

"And I know you! You are — Humphrey van Weyden," she said. "But why are you here? Do you hope to write a story about the sea?"

"Certainly not," he replied. "I'm no story-teller."

They talked on and on. They talked about what she wrote and about other books. They forgot about everyone else.

For Humphrey, the next few days were wonderful. He talked to Maud whenever he could. She was pretty and gentle and she seemed to respect him both as a man and a writer. He was falling in love with her.

The captain's eyes followed Maud, too.

Suddenly, there was trouble. A ship called the *Macedonia* was close by. Its captain was Death Larsen, Wolf's brother. Each day, its hunting boats went out and stayed close to the *Ghost's* hunting boats. Their hunters were getting the seals Wolf's men should have taken.

Wolf was angry. He would not let his brother get away with this!

The *Ghost* and her hunting boats followed the other hunters. They caught up with them. They forced the men to come on the *Ghost*. They pulled the boats up on deck.

Death saw what was happening. He steered his ship for the *Ghost*. But Wolf was too clever for him. A fog was rolling in. The *Ghost* headed into it. Before the *Macedonia* could catch up, the *Ghost* was lost in the fog.

Wolf was pleased. Now he had more hunters and more boats than ever. "That will teach my brother to respect me! Bring out the whiskey!" he said. "Whiskey for everyone!"

All the men drank. The hunters and the sailors drank. The men from the *Macedonia* drank. Humphrey watched them. There was little happiness. The men from the *Ghost* told terrible stories about Wolf, talked of fights and beatings on the ship, told of the men who had died. It was a wild, sad party.

The captain didn't drink. After supper, he, Maud, and Humphrey went up on deck where they could see the *Macedonia's* lights.

"What if I called out to them?" Humphrey asked.

"I would break your neck," Wolf replied.

"And if *I* cried out?" Maud asked.

"I like you too much to hurt *you*," said Wolf, "but I would have to break Mr. van Weyden's neck."

MAUD

COMPREHENSION CHECK

Choose the best answer.

1. Wolf Larsen told Maud they would reach Japan
   _____a. in three or four weeks.
   _____b. in three or four months.
   _____c. when the hunt was over.
   _____d. when all the seals had been killed.

2. When Maud learned how long they might be at sea, she
   _____a. cried.
   _____b. argued.
   _____c. was pleased.
   _____d. refused to eat.

3. Maud worked for a living. She was a
   _____a. movie star.
   _____b. teacher.
   _____c. writer.
   _____d. cook.

4. Maud Brewster
   _____a. was a well-known person.
   _____b. was not liked very much.
   _____c. did not have many friends.
   _____d. did not like Humphrey.

5. Wolf Larsen's brother's ship was called
   _____a. the *Macaroni* II.
   _____b. the *Macadamia*.
   _____c. the *Mackerel*.
   _____d. the *Macedonia*.

6. Wolf Larsen was angry with his brother because
   _____a. his hunters were taking the seals that Wolf's men should have taken.
   _____b. he had a bigger ship than Wolf.
   _____c. his men were better hunters than Wolf's.
   _____d. he had made a name for himself.

7. What was Wolf Larsen's brother's name?
   _____a. Dollar Larsen
   _____b. Death Larsen
   _____c. Drew Larsen
   _____d. Daniel Larsen

8. Wolf Larsen
   _____a. did not like the idea of having a woman on board.
   _____b. had a soft spot in his heart for Maud Brewster.
   _____c. did not care for Maud's writings.
   _____d. wanted Maud to write a book about the *Ghost*.

9. Another name for this story could be
   _____a. "Party Time."
   _____b. "Humphrey Falls in Love."
   _____c. "More Trouble at Sea."
   _____d. "The Story-teller."

10. This story is mainly about
   _____a. a sea captain who fears no one.
   _____b. Maud Brewster's days at sea.
   _____c. Humphrey's love for Maud Brewster.
   _____d. Wolf's respect for his brother.

Check your answers with the key on page 67.

MAUD

VOCABULARY CHECK

| certainly | gentle | happiness | joy | respect | wrote |

I. Sentences to Finish

Fill in the blank in each sentence with the correct key word from the box above.

1. Everyone has_____for Lilly because she is so kind.

2. Kate is so helpful around the house that she is a_____to her mother.

3. The new baby brought so much_____to the family.

4. Doug_____me a letter while he was away.

5. If we don't hurry, we'll_____be late for the show.

6. The little child gave the kitten a_____hug.

II. Word Search

Use the key words from the box above to fill in the puzzle. They may be written from left to right, or up and down. One word, that is not a key word, has been done for you.

```
E  W  S  P  E  C  W  L  K  B
F  R  E  S  P  E  C  T  W  E
J  O  Y  F  C  J  E  H  J  L
A  T  R  E  J  O  R  A  C  O
K  E  F  G  E  N  T  L  E  S
C  E  R  T  A  P  A  X  N  E
Z  A  J  O  N  P  I  C  U  Y
U  H  A  P  P  I  N  E  S  S
M  E  W  R  O  T  L  C  S  Z
A  G  H  A  P  E  Y  G  Z  A
```

Check your answers with the key on page 71.

This page may be reproduced for classroom use.

The Island

PREPARATION

Key Words

island	(i´ lənd)	land surrounded by water *Joan landed her boat on a small <u>island</u>.*
prepare	(pri pãr´)	make ready *<u>Prepare</u> to leave tomorrow morning.*
raise	(rāz)	to lift; to pull or push up *Help me <u>raise</u> the sail on my boat.*
saving	(sāv´ ing)	rescuing; taking out of danger *Matt was proud of his dog for <u>saving</u> the drowning child.*
tire	(tīr)	to wear out; wear down *After two hours of working, he began to <u>tire</u>.*
wore	(wôr)	put on; dressed up in *Jack <u>wore</u> his new shoes to school.*

The Island

Necessary Words

bail(ed)   (bāl)   to take water out of a boat with some kind of container
> *As the boat took on water, we had to <u>bail</u> it out.*

cove   (cōv)   a small bay
> *The ships stayed in the <u>cove</u> until the storm passed.*

gun   (gun)   a tool used for hunting
> *John took his <u>gun</u> with him when he went into the woods.*

load(ed)   (lōd)   to pack; to put things into place
> *We <u>loaded</u> the boat with food for our picnic on the island.*

sick   (sik)   ill; not well
> *Betty was so <u>sick</u> she had to stay in bed.*

trust   (trust)   to have faith in; believe in
> *My parents <u>trust</u> me to take care of my brothers and sisters.*

The Island

Maud struggles to free herself from Wolf Larsen's arms.

Preview:
1. Read the name of the story.
2. Look at the picture.
3. Read the sentence under the picture.
4. Read the first four paragraphs of the story.
5. Then answer the following question.

You learned from your preview that Maud Brewster
___a. was in love with Humphrey.
___b. was in love with Wolf Larsen.
___c. had a great respect for Wolf Larsen.
___d. was frightened by Wolf Larsen.

Turn to the Comprehension Check on page 58 for the right answer.

Now read the story.

Read to find out what happens when Wolf Larsen becomes ill.

The Island

That evening, Humphrey woke up suddenly and sat up in his bunk, listening. It was Maud's voice, and she sounded frightened.

He hurried to her cabin, opened the door, and saw Wolf Larsen holding her. She was trying to get away from him.

Humphrey ran at the captain, but Wolf threw him off as if he weighed nothing.

Humphrey thought of all the captain had done to him, had done to others. And now, this! He pulled out his knife.

And then — something very strange happened. Wolf let Maud go, and put his hands to his head. He seemed terribly sick.

At this, Humphrey stopped. Then it all came back again. Wolf Larsen was a murderer! It was time for him to die.

Humphrey began to raise his knife to strike.

"No, don't!" cried Maud.

Humphrey stopped. The captain's hand was over his eyes.

"Help me to a seat!" Wolf said. "I am a sick man, Mr. van Weyden, a very sick man."

Humphrey helped him back to his stateroom. The captain fell into his bunk. "It's my head," he kept saying, "I am a sick man, I am a very sick man."

When Humphrey asked Maud what had happened, she didn't know. "He just let go of me," she said.

"We must think about saving ourselves," Humphrey said. "He can't hurt us now. But later, when he's better, I'm afraid he will. Saving our lives means we must prepare to leave the *Ghost*. Do you trust me?"

"Yes," said Maud.

"Then go to your cabin and bring back anything you will need. Dress warmly — and hurry!" he said.

He took food, water, and oilskins from the ship's store, and he took Wolf's gun from his stateroom. The captain was still in his bunk. Maud helped as much as she could to prepare what they needed. Humphrey knew she would quickly tire, so he told her to rest while he loaded the boat.

He lowered the boat into the water and rowed them out, away from the *Ghost*. Then he raised the sail. "We're going to Japan," he told Maud. "We'll be there in five days, with good weather."

"If it storms? What then?" Maud asked.

"We may be picked up by another ship," Humphrey said.

Day broke, gray and cold. Maud wore the warm shirt Humphrey brought for her and she wore a man's cap to cover her hair. They had a cold breakfast.

Steering was hard, and Humphrey tired after a few hours. Maud said she would learn how to steer, so he could rest. He fell asleep. When he woke, the wind had

changed. It was blowing them back to the *Ghost*. He took down the sails.

Night came. Maud bravely took her turn as the look-out, while Humphrey slept. That was the end of their first day at sea.

There were more days, many more days. There were storms and high winds. Waves broke over the boat, filling it with water. Maud and Humphrey bailed for hours at a time. Then fog rolled in. The two were tired, wet, and cold. It seemed that their journey would never end.

Then, one day, Humphrey saw land. They were headed for an island — and for the rocks around it. If they hit the rocks, the boat would almost certainly break up, and neither of them could swim.

"We must go around the rocks," Humphrey said.

Maud put her hand into his. "Humphrey, thank you for everything," she said.

Humphrey thought, "She is saying good-bye." Maud did not believe they would make it to land.

"We are not going to die," he said. They had not come this far just to drown!

The waves carried them on, past the rocks to the island. The boat came to rest in a tiny cove. They had reached land. They were safe at last!

The Island

COMPREHENSION CHECK

Choose the best answer.

Preview Answer:

d. was frightened by Wolf Larsen.

1. Seeing that Maud needed help, Humphrey went after Wolf Larsen. When Wolf threw him aside, Humphrey
   _____a. pulled out his knife.
   _____b. pulled out his gun.
   _____c. called out for the other men to help him.
   _____d. told Maud to make a run for it!

2. Just as Humphrey raised his weapon to Wolf,
   _____a. Maud suddenly became sick.
   _____b. Humphrey suddenly became sick.
   _____c. Maud cried out and stopped Humphrey from striking Wolf.
   _____d. Wolf passed out.

3. Maud didn't want Humphrey to kill the captain because
   _____a. she loved Wolf.
   _____b. she could see that Wolf was sick.
   _____c. she felt sorry for Wolf.
   _____d. she didn't like the sight of blood.

4. Now that the captain was sick,
   _____a. Humphrey threw a party for everyone.
   _____b. Humphrey put himself in charge of the ship.
   _____c. Humphrey steered the *Ghost* toward land.
   _____d. Humphrey and Maud prepared to leave the *Ghost*.

5. As Humphrey lowered the boat into the water, he told Maud that they would sail for
   _____a. America.
   _____b. Africa.
   _____c. Japan.
   _____d. Canada.

6. Maud learned how to steer so that Humphrey could rest. She also took her turn as look-out. This tells us that Maud was
   _____a. a brave woman.
   _____b. a strong woman.
   _____c. a silly woman.
   _____d. a frightened woman.

7. Maud's and Humphrey's days at sea
   _____a. were filled with wonder.
   _____b. were a time of real happiness.
   _____c. were very merry.
   _____d. were very hard.

8. Maud believed
   _____a. they would get lost in a storm.
   _____b. they would die of thirst.
   _____c. they would make it to Japan.
   _____d. they would never make it to land.

9. Another name for this story could be
   _____a. "A Time to Die."
   _____b. "Leaving Ship."
   _____c. "The Rescue."
   _____d. "A Journey that Would Not End."

10. This story is mainly about
    _____a. how Maud saved Humphrey's life and her own.
    _____b. how Maud and Humphrey made it to land.
    _____c. how Wolf Larsen became sick.
    _____d. how Maud learned to steer a boat.

Check your answers with the key on page 67.

This page may be reproduced for classroom use.

The Island

VOCABULARY CHECK

island	prepare	raise	saving	tire	wore

I. Sentences to Finish

Fill in the blank in each sentence with the correct key word from the box above.

1. I_____my new dress to the party on Saturday.

2. Mother will_____lunch for the picnic tomorrow.

3. Grandpa Jarrett lives on the_____of Hawaii.

4. It's Paul's turn to_____the flag today.

5. Brave firemen around the world are_____lives every day.

6. Jack began to_____from running so fast, so he dropped out of the race.

II. Read each sentence. Then find which key word beneath it could be used instead of the underlined word or words. Circle the letter in front of the correct word.

1. It would be nice to live on an <u>land surrounded by water</u> of your own.
       a. ocean   b. island   c. orange   d. animal

2. Dad will <u>make ready</u> breakfast for Mom on her day off.
       a. pocket   b. paint   c. plant   d. prepare

3. Don <u>put on</u> his new suit to the party.
       a. wore   b. washed   c. watered   d. welcomed

4. <u>Lift, pull, or push up</u> your hand if you know the answer.
       a. Remember   b. Return   c. Raise   d. Rock

5. Shovel slowly, and you won't <u>wear out</u> so fast.
       a. tire   b. think   c. trip   d. turn

6. She thanked the man for <u>taking out of danger</u> her life.
       a. starting   b. slowing   c. saving   d. sending

Check your answers with the key on page 71

The End of the Sea Wolf

PREPARATION

Key Words

kiss	(kis)	to touch someone with the lips in a loving way *Humphrey wanted to <u>kiss</u> Maud.*
leak	(lēk)	to let water come through *The boat started to <u>leak</u> and we thought it would sink.*
match	(match)	a tiny stick with a chemical on the tip, used for lighting fires *Jed used a <u>match</u> to start the fire.*
needle	(nē´ dl)	a small, sharp tool used for sewing *She used a <u>needle</u> to sew up my pants.*
softly	(soft´ lē)	faintly or quietly *Danny talked <u>softly</u> to the frightened dog.*
somebody	(sum´ bod ē)	some person not named *Will <u>somebody</u> turn off the light and shut the door?*

The End of the Sea Wolf

Necessary Words

body   (bod´ ē)   the whole part of a man or animal
                                   The sailor's <u>body</u> lay on the deck.

chest   (chest)   a large box, often made of wood, used to store clothes and other things
                                   The sailor put his oilskins in his sea <u>chest</u>.

handcuff (ed) (hand´ kuf)   metal bonds or chains used to keep someone from using his or her hands
                                   They <u>handcuffed</u> the man before taking him away.

hut   (hut)   a small, simple house with one or two rooms
                                   Billy and his brother built a <u>hut</u> in the woods.

The End of the Sea Wolf

For the first time in weeks, Maud and Humphrey enjoy a hot meal.

Preview: 1. Read the name of the story.
2. Look at the picture.
3. Read the sentence under the picture.
4. Read the first two paragraphs of the story.
5. Then answer the following question.

You learned from your preview that when Humphrey left the Ghost, he forgot to bring along

___a. food.
___b. water.
___c. warm blankets.
___d. matches.

Turn to the Comprehension Check on page 64 for the right answer.

Now read the story.

Read to find out what lands on the island one morning.

The End of the Sea Wolf

"I need a match," Humphrey said. "We could have a fire. I can't believe I forgot the matches."

Then he had an idea. He used one of the gun shells to start the fire. Soon he had a roaring fire — and hot coffee. For the first time in weeks, Maud and Humphrey had a hot meal.

The next day, they sailed around the island, hoping to find somebody living there, but there were no houses or people.

"We must prepare to winter here," Humphrey said softly. They would not be rescued, after all.

Together they built a tiny hut with walls made of wood. But what about the roof? A wood roof would leak. They hunted seals and skinned them. Maud used her needle to sew the skins together.

"It smells, but it won't leak," she said. They would be warm and dry when winter came.

Humphrey was so proud of Maud. How he loved this brave, beautiful lady! He longed to kiss and hold her, and he hoped that she cared for him, too.

Then, one morning, Humphrey saw the *Ghost*! The ship had landed on their island. She was broken, her sails down. Humphrey boarded, taking his gun.

There was no sign of the men. Surely, somebody was still on the ship.

Then he saw Wolf.

He raised the gun, but he couldn't bring himself to kill the captain.

"What happened here?" Humphrey asked.

Wolf replied, "My brother boarded the ship one evening. The men followed him to the *Macedonia* and Cooky cut the rigging before they left. So here I am, alone on the *Ghost*."

The captain seemed very sick.

Humphrey left him and went inside the ship. He took food and some cups and, just to be safe, he took Wolf's guns, too. He returned to the hut to prepare breakfast.

The meal was ready when Maud came out. She saw the *Ghost*.

She asked softly, "Is he __?"

"He is," said Humphrey.

Humphrey boarded the ship again, but did not see Wolf. He opened a trap door on deck to get some things he and Maud needed.

When he heard the captain coming, he hid. Wolf did not see the open trap door, and almost fell in. Then he quickly closed the door. He went away and brought back a sea chest and placed it over the trap door.

Now, Humphrey knew: *Wolf could not see.* The captain thought he had caught Humphrey under the door.

Later, Humphrey talked to Maud about an idea he had. "I'm going to fix the *Ghost*. She'll take us home!"

They brought the *Ghost's* sails to land and Maud got busy with her needle, mending. When Humphrey started work on the rigging, Wolf came outside.

"I'm fixing your boat," Humphrey said.

"I won't let you," said the captain.

Humphrey laughed. "You can't stop me. Don't you want to leave this island?"

"No," the captain said. "I expect to die here."

"Well, we don't," said Humphrey.

He and Maud moved back on the ship. They would stay out of Wolf's way.

The captain tried to stop their work on his ship. First, he hid the masts, then he tried to cut the rigging. Humphrey handcuffed him to his bunk, but the captain would not stop trying. He tried to set the ship on fire and, after that, he was too sick to do anything more.

The blind Wolf became sicker every day until he could no longer walk, hear, or talk. He was all alone with himself. He could hurt no one any more.

At last, the *Ghost* was ready. They set off — into a storm. Humphrey steered the ship through wind and high waves, until he could do no more. He fell into his bunk and slept.

He woke to find that Wolf had died.

Humphrey and Maud dropped the body into the sea. The Sea Wolf was no more.

As they stood watching the body sink below the waves, they saw a ship.

"Look — we are saved!" Humphrey said. His arms went about Maud. She raised her face, and they kissed. At last, they were going home.

The End of the Sea Wolf

COMPREHENSION CHECK

Choose the best answer.

1. Maud and Humphrey sailed around the island hoping to find
   _____a. a match.
   _____b. some fruit.
   _____c. a passing ship.
   _____d. some people.

2. Maud and Humphrey found

   _____a. many houses on the island.
   _____b. no one living on the island.
   _____c. many people on the island.
   _____d. many animals on the island.

3. Learning that they would not be rescued, Maud and Humphrey

   _____a. prepared for the winter.
   _____b. prepared for the long, hot summer.
   _____c. planted seeds to grow vegetables.
   _____d. built a bigger boat.

4. Together, Maud and Humphrey built a hut made of wood. What did they use for a roof?

   _____a. Seal skins sewn together
   _____b. Large leaves sewn together
   _____c. Dried mud
   _____d. Paper

5. Maud and Humphrey

   _____a. settled down to a lonely life together.
   _____b. knew they would die on the island.
   _____c. never gave up hope of being rescued.
   _____d. had many animal friends.

6. When Humphrey spotted the *Ghost* on the island, he went aboard and found Wolf Larsen
   _____a. singing, and drinking whiskey.
   _____b. all alone, and happy about it.
   _____c. lonely and frightened.
   _____d. blind, and all alone.

7. Humphrey's idea was to
   _____a. kill Wolf Larsen and steal the *Ghost*.
   _____b. sink the *Ghost*, and the captain with it.
   _____c. fix the *Ghost* and send Wolf Larsen on his way.
   _____d. fix the *Ghost* to take them home.

8. When Wolf Larsen died, Humphrey and Maud
   _____a. buried his body.
   _____b. burned his body.
   _____c. dropped his body into the sea.
   _____d. fed his body to the hungry seals.

9. Another name for this story could be
   _____a. "Rescued At Last!"
   _____b. "Winter on the Island."
   _____c. "Death Larsen Gets Even."
   _____d. "Buried At Sea."

10. This story is mainly about
    _____a. how Wolf Larsen's brother got even with him.
    _____b. Humphrey's love for Maud.
    _____c. how Wolf Larsen died.
    _____d. how hard work, hope, and a little luck, saved the lives of Maud and Humphrey.

Check your answers with the key on page 67.

This page may be reproduced for classroom use.

The End of the Sea Wolf

VOCABULARY CHECK

kiss	leak	match	needle	softly	somebody

I. Sentences to Finish

Fill in the blank in each sentence with the correct key word from the box above.

1. I always remember to_____Mother good-bye before I leave the house.

2. I know that_____has been into the cookie jar.

3. Lisa speaks so_____, that no one can hear her.

4. The sharp_____went right through Mother's finger.

5. The washing machine began to_____water all over the floor.

6. The_____was wet and would not light.

II. Matching

Write the letter of the correct meaning from Column B next to the key word in Column A.

Column A

_____1. needle

_____2. kiss

_____3. somebody

_____4. leak

_____5. softly

_____6. match

Column B

a. some person not named

b. to let water come through

c. faintly or quietly

d. a small, sharp tool used for sewing

e. a tiny stick used for lighting fires

f. to touch someone with the lips in a loving way

Check your answers with the key on page 72.

This page may be reproduced for classroom use.

NOTES

COMPREHENSION CHECK PROGRESS CHART
Lessons CTR C-61 to CTR C-70

LESSON NUMBER	QUESTION NUMBER										PAGE NUMBER
	1	2	3	4	5	6	7	8	9	10	
CTR C-61	d	b	(c)	c	a	b	d	c	△a	[c]	10
CTR C-62	b	d	(b)	a	c	c	a	b	△b	[c]	16
CTR C-63	(b)	(a)	c	c	d	b	(b)	d	△a	[b]	22
CTR C-64	(a)	(c)	b	(d)	b	d	a	b	△c	[a]	28
CTR C-65	c	(d)	c	a	b	(d)	(a)	(d)	△a	[a]	34
CTR C-66	(d)	b	a	c	b	d	c	a	△a	[d]	40
CTR C-67	b	a	d	a	c	(d)	(a)	(c)	△a	[a]	46
CTR C-68	c	b	c	(a)	d	a	b	(b)	△c	[a]	52
CTR C-69	a	c	(b)	d	c	(a)	(d)	d	△b	[b]	58
CTR C-70	d	b	a	a	(c)	d	d	c	△a	[d]	64

◯ = Inference (not said straight out, but you know from what is said)

△ = Another name for the story

▢ = Main idea of the story

NOTES

VOCABULARY CHECK ANSWER KEY
Lessons CTR C-61 to CTR C-70

61   **OUT OF THE FOG**   **11**

I. 1. faint
2. journey
3. deck
4. fog
5. passenger
6. rescue

II.

```
                          ¹P
                    ¹F A I N T
                          S
                          S              ²D
                    ²R E S C U E
                          N              C
              ³F        G              K
          ³J O U R N E Y
              G        R
```

62   **THE CABIN BOY**   **17**

I. 1. sailor
2. course
3. force
4. cabin
5. lesson
6. learn

II.

```
L E S S O N C A B
E C O U F S A I L
S A I L O R A B E
S C O U R S E L A
C A B E C A B I N
F O R L E A R N F
```

63   **MISSING MONEY**   **23**

I. 1. pot
2. expect
3. reply
4. fellow
5. lie
6. neither

II. 1. f
2. a
3. d
4. e
5. c
6. b

VOCABULARY CHECK ANSWER KEY
Lessons CTR C-61 to CTR C-70

64 COOKY   **29**

I. 1. drank
      2. wouldn't
      3. sharp
      4. repeat
      5. knife
      6. strike

65 THE NEW MATE   **35**

I. 1. You've   *II.* 1. b
      2. shape   2. b
      3. ocean   3. b
      4. slept   4. b
      5. bunk   5. b
      6. search   6. b

66 THE HUNT   **41**

I. 1. slide   *II.* 1. slide, c
      2. sail   2. tumble, f
      3. spray   3. coffee, e
      4. coffee   4. curl, a
      5. tumble   5. spray, d
      6. curl   6. sail, b

VOCABULARY CHECK ANSWER KEY
Lessons CTR C-61 to CTR C-70

67   LOST   **47**

I. 1. breeze
   2. weather
   3. sank
   4. welcome
   5. steer
   6. trap

II.

```
K  S  T  E  E  P  S  A  N  D
I  B  R  O  W  G  A  R  J  A
W  S  A  W  E  L  L  M  B  B
S  T  P  E  E  X  E  D  R  W
A  E  X  L  S  A  N  K  E  E
V  E  U  C  Q  Z  T  T  E  L
I  R  N  O  C  H  O  H  Z  C
X  W  E  M  L  B  R  E  E  Q
R  Q  S  E  P  T  R  E  E  R
```

68   MAUD   **53**

I. 1. respect
   2. joy
   3. happiness/joy
   4. wrote
   5. certainly
   6. gentle

II.

```
E  W  S  P  E  C  W  L  K  B
F  R  E  S  P  E  C  T  W  E
J  O  Y  F  C  J  E  H  J  L
A  T  R  E  J  O  R  A  C  O
K  E  F  G  E  N  T  L  E  S
C  E  R  T  A  P  A  X  N  E
Z  A  J  O  N  P  I  C  U  Y
U  H  A  P  P  I  N  E  S  S
M  E  W  R  O  T  L  C  S  Z
A  G  H  A  P  E  Y  G  Z  A
```

69   THE ISLAND   **59**

I. 1. wore
   2. prepare
   3. island
   4. raise
   5. saving
   6. tire

II. 1. b
   2. d
   3. a
   4. c
   5. a
   6. c

VOCABULARY CHECK ANSWER KEY
Lessons CTR C-61 to CTR C-70

LESSON
NUMBER

PAGE
NUMBER

70   **THE END OF THE SEA WOLF**   **65**

I. 1. kiss   *II.* 1. d
      2. somebody   2. f
      3. softly   3. a
      4. needle   4. b
      5. leak   5. c
      6. match   6. e